SPORTS GREAT EMMITT SMITH

—Sports Great Books—

BASEBALL

Sports Great Jim Abbott
0-89490-395-0/ Savage

Sports Great Barry Bonds
0-89490-595-3/ Sullivan

Sports Great Bobby Bonilla
0-89490-417-5/ Knapp

Sports Great Orel Hershiser
0-89490-389-6/ Knapp

Sports Great Bo Jackson
0-89490-281-4/ Knapp

Sports Great Greg Maddux
0-89490-873-1/ Thornley

Sports Great Kirby Puckett
0-89490-392-6/ Aaseng

Sports Great Cal Ripken, Jr.
0-89490-387-X/ Macnow

Sports Great Nolan Ryan
0-89490-394-2/ Lace

Sports Great Darryl Strawberry
0-89490-291-1/ Torres & Sullivan

BASKETBALL

**Sports Great Charles Barkley
Revised Edition**
0-7660-1004-X/ Macnow

Sports Great Larry Bird
0-89490-368-3/ Kavanagh

Sports Great Muggsy Bogues
0-89490-876-6/ Rekela

Sports Great Patrick Ewing
0-89490-369-1/ Kavanagh

Sports Great Anfernee Hardaway
0-89490-758-1/ Rekela

**Sports Great Magic Johnson
Revised and Expanded**
0-89490-348-9/ Haskins

**Sports Great Michael Jordan
Revised Edition**
0-89490-978-9/ Aaseng

Sports Great Jason Kidd
0-7660-1001-5/ Torres

Sports Great Karl Malone
0-89490-599-6/ Savage

Sports Great Reggie Miller
0-89490-874-X/ Thornley

Sports Great Alonzo Mourning
0-89490-875-8/ Fortunato

Sports Great Hakeem Olajuwon
0-89490-372-1/ Knapp

**Sports Great Shaquille O'Neal
Revised Edition**
0-7660-1003-1/ Sullivan

Sports Great Scottie Pippen
0-89490-755-7/ Bjarkman

**Sports Great David Robinson
Revised Edition**
0-7660-1077-5/ Aaseng

Sports Great Dennis Rodman
0-89490-759-X/ Thornley

Sports Great John Stockton
0-89490-598-8/ Aaseng

Sports Great Isiah Thomas
0-89490-374-8/ Knapp

Sports Great Dominique Wilkins
0-89490-754-9/ Bjarkman

FOOTBALL

Sports Great Troy Aikman
0-89490-593-7/ Macnow

Sports Great Jerome Bettis
0-89490-872-3/Majewski

Sports Great John Elway
0-89490-282-2/ Fox

Sports Great Brett Favre
0-7660-1000-7/ Savage

Sports Great Jim Kelly
0-89490-670-4/ Harrington

Sports Great Joe Montana
0-89490-371-3/ Kavanagh

Sports Great Jerry Rice
0-89490-419-1/ Dickey

Sports Great Barry Sanders
0-89490-418-3/ Knapp

Sports Great Emmitt Smith
0-7660-1002-3/ Grabowski

Sports Great Herschel Walker
0-89490-207-5/ Benagh

HOCKEY

Sports Great Wayne Gretzky
0-89490-757-3/ Rappoport

Sports Great Mario Lemieux
0-89490-596-1/ Knapp

Sports Great Eric Lindros
0-89490-871-5/ Rappoport

TENNIS

Sports Great Steffi Graf
0-89490-597-X/ Knapp

Sports Great Pete Sampras
0-89490-756-5/ Sherrow

SPORTS GREAT EMMITT SMITH

John Grabowski

—Sports Great Books—

E **Enslow Publishers, Inc.**
44 Fadem Road   PO Box 38
Box 699   Aldershot
Springfield, NJ 07081   Hants GU12 6BP
USA   UK

Library of Congress Cataloging-in-Publication Data

Grabowski, John F.
    Sports great Emmitt Smith / John Grabowski.
       p. cm. — (Sports great books)
    Includes index.
    Summary: Profiles the personal life and football career of the All-Pro running back with the Dallas Cowboys, Emmitt Smith.
    ISBN 0-7660-1002-3
    1. Smith, Emmitt, 1969– —Juvenile literature. 2. Football players—United States—Biography—Juvenile literature. 3. Dallas Cowboys (Football team)—Juvenile literature. [1. Smith, Emmitt, 1969– . 2. Football players. 3. Afro-Americans—Biography.] I. Title. II. Series.
GV939.S635G73 1998
796.332'092—dc21
    [B]   97-27216
                                                    CIP
                                                        AC

Printed in the United States of America

10 9 8 7 6 5 4 3 2 1

Illustration Credits: Layne Murdoch Photos, pp. 8, 11, 12, 15, 18, 21, 24, 26, 29, 32, 35, 36, 39, 42, 44, 47, 49, 52, 57, 60.

Cover Illustration: Layne Murdoch Photos.

Contents

Chapter 1

The 1993 season was a memorable one for the Dallas Cowboys. Interestingly enough, the year began on a bitter note. Star running back Emmitt Smith was engaged in a bitter contract dispute with Cowboys owner Jerry Jones. The negotiations were still dragging on as the regular season got under way. Without Smith, Dallas lost its first two games. Team morale was at a low point. The players themselves knew how important Smith was to the team. "We're nothing without him," said center Mark Stepnoski. Jones finally raised his offer, and Smith signed.

With Smith in uniform, the Cowboys were a different team. They went on to win the Eastern Division title in the National Football Conference (NFC) of the National Football League (NFL). Smith won the league's rushing title for the third consecutive year. For his efforts, he was named the league's Most Valuable Player (MVP). It was an incredible feat for a five-foot nine-inch running back playing in a league of giants.

In the final game of the year, however, Smith was

Emmitt Smith walks off the field with wide receivers Michael Irvin (#88), and Alvin Harper (#80).

seriously injured. Playing against the New York Giants, he separated his shoulder. Wide receiver Alvin Harper reported the pain Smith was suffering. "In the huddle, you could see his eyes watering," said Harper. "I asked him how he felt and he said, 'Man, you don't want to know.'"

Despite the pain, Smith's loyalty to his teammates kept him in the game. It was one of the qualities instilled in him by his strong family upbringing. "You have players relying on you," he said. "I didn't want to let them down." He didn't. He led the Cowboys to a 16–13 overtime victory. The win gave Dallas a week off before the playoffs began. Smith began physical therapy on the shoulder immediately after the game.

The team ran over the Green Bay Packers and San Francisco 49ers in the playoffs. Smith played, but pain shot through his entire body. In spite of that, opposing teams knew Smith was the man who had to be stopped. "I still think you can beat them, first by taking away Emmitt," said San Francisco cornerback Eric Davis. "You've got to concern yourself about him." That became the problem facing the Buffalo Bills. The Bills would be the Cowboys' opponent in Super Bowl XXVIII.

"Is Emmitt O.K.?" asked 49er tight end Jamie Williams after the San Francisco game. "He'll be fine," said a writer. "Then Buffalo's in trouble," responded Williams. Williams proved to be right.

The site for the game was the Georgia Dome in Atlanta, Georgia. The date was January 30, 1994. Dallas stood on the brink of winning its second consecutive league championship.

To make matters worse for Dallas, quarterback Troy Aikman had suffered a concussion in the San Francisco game. Since Smith was still nursing his injury, the Cowboys were forced to play the biggest game of the year with two of their offensive stars at less than full strength.

The Buffalo Bills were a formidable opponent. They were appearing in the Super Bowl for the fourth consecutive year. No other team had ever played in the game four straight years. The Cowboys knew they had their work cut out for them. Buffalo had lost the previous three Super Bowls. The Bills wanted to break their losing streak and win their first Super Bowl championship.

Dallas won the coin toss at the start of the game. They received the opening kickoff and went on to score a field goal. Aside from that, however, Buffalo dominated the first two quarters of play. When the teams left the field at halftime, Buffalo had a 13–6 lead. The Cowboys' offense could not seem to mount an attack.

Offensive coordinator Norv Turner knew what had to be done in the second half. "Emmitt came up to me at halftime and said, 'Norv, you've got to get the ball into my hands,' and I do what Emmitt tells me," related Turner. "We had to establish Emmitt in the second half, and we had to do it with power." And do it they did.

Buffalo had the ball to start the third quarter. On the third play from scrimmage, Thurman Thomas fumbled. Safety James Washington recovered for Dallas. He ran the ball back 46 yards for the touchdown, which tied the game.

After Dallas stopped Buffalo once again, the Cowboys took over on their own 36-yard line. Dallas turned to Smith seven times in the next eight plays. Smith ran for a total of 61 yards on the drive. On the last play, he scored on a 15-yard run to give the Cowboys a 20–13 lead.

The Cowboys never looked back. They proceeded to score 24 points in the half while holding Buffalo scoreless. Smith scored on another run at the start of the fourth quarter. All told, he gained 132 yards rushing for the day on 30 carries. To do this while nursing a separated shoulder was incredible.

Emmitt Smith is mobbed by teammate Michael Irvin and the Dallas Cowboys' mascot after Smith scored a touchdown in Super Bowl XXVIII.

Emmitt Smith kisses the Vince Lombardi Trophy during the postgame celebration. He is holding up two fingers to symbolize the Cowboys' back-to-back world championships.

The game wound down, and the Cowboys began their victory celebration. Smith received word that he had been named the Most Valuable Player of the Super Bowl. Even at such a moment of personal triumph, Smith was thinking of his teammates. "I wish," he said, "there was some way they could have given co-awards so James Washington could have gotten something."

The award was the crowning touch to an amazing season. Cowboys owner Jerry Jones began to have second thoughts on the contract he gave Smith. "Maybe we got a bargain," he mused. He knew for a fact that he had something special in Emmitt Smith.

Chapter 2

It didn't take the Smith family of Pensacola, Florida, long to realize that football would be an important part of young Emmitt J. Smith III's life. When he was just a few months old, his mother placed him on his swing in front of the television. When a football game came on, the youngster stopped fidgeting. He followed the action on the screen with his eyes. Perhaps the interest in the game was only natural. Emmitt's father—Emmitt Jr.—had been a high-school gridiron star some years before.

As Emmitt grew older, everything seemed to revolve around football. "I remember it before anything else," he says today. "Sitting there watching, wanting to play. It's my earliest memory. Before anything else, there was football."

Although the sport was the most important thing in his life, his parents made sure he realized it was not the only thing. Emmitt's father was a city bus driver. With five children to feed and clothe, money did not come easily for the family. The children were taught the value of hard work

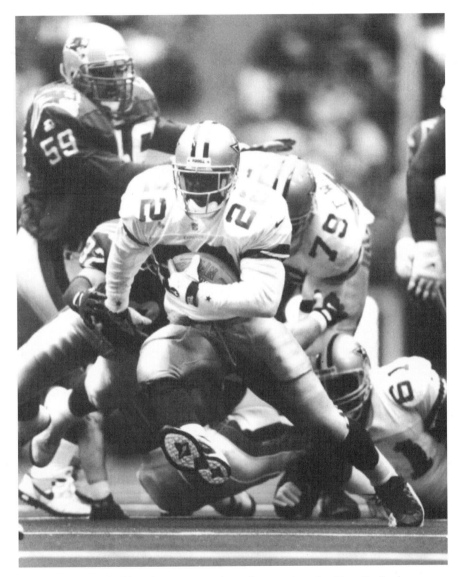

Emmitt Smith gains some tough yardage against the New England Patriots. Smith learned from his parents to work hard at an early age; a lesson that he has never forgotten.

at an early age. Young Emmitt ran errands to earn money, which he then saved to buy himself clothes.

At age eight, Emmitt got his first taste of organized football. He was large for his age, and dominated most games he played in. His first position was quarterback, then running back. The Mini-Mites, Mites, and Midget leagues were the training grounds where he developed his moves. He would thrill Cowboys fans with them years later.

The Brownsville Middle School that he attended did not have a football team. Emmitt ran track and played basketball. He was good enough on the court to help the school win the city championship in basketball when he was in seventh grade. Emmitt continued to play football in the youth leagues. By the time he was ready for high school, he had gained a reputation as a player to watch.

The new coach at Escambia High that year was Dwight Thomas. He had been hired to turn around the school's football program. Over the previous eighteen years, Escambia recorded only one winning season. The year before Emmitt arrived, Escambia was 1–9. Coach Thomas became a strong influence on Emmitt. He reinforced the values of hard work and discipline that had been taught by Emmitt's parents. Said Thomas, "I told the team that I only had three rules: Be where you're supposed to be; be there when you're supposed to be there; and be doing what you're supposed to be doing. That was Emmitt."

As a five-foot eight-inch, 175-pound freshman, Emmitt gave hints of things to come. In his very first game, he rushed for 115 yards and scored two touchdowns against Pensacola Catholic High. Escambia finished with a 7–3 record. It was an improvement of six games over the previous year.

That improvement continued through Emmitt's sophomore season. The school made the state playoffs after compiling a 12–2 record. Escambia defeated Bartow High to become the class 3-A champions of the state of Florida. By the time Emmitt was a junior, Escambia had gone from laughingstock to powerhouse. The school moved up to class 4-A, and Smith became the most feared runner in the district. "We do three things here on offense," said Coach Thomas. "We hand the ball to Emmitt, we pitch the ball to Emmitt, and we throw the ball to Emmitt."

Working out with weights made him even more powerful than before. He rushed for 200 or more yards seven times that season, with a high of 301 yards against Milton High School. Emmitt led his team to a 13–1 record, and another state championship. This time, Escambia defeated Bradenton Southeast High for the crown.

Emmitt's senior year was a bit of a letdown. It didn't end with another championship. A 9–1 record was not good enough to win the team a spot in the playoffs. His performance on the field, however, earned him "High School Player of the Year" honors from *Parade* magazine.

Emmitt's statistics for his four years of school were mind-boggling. He had rushed for a total of 8,804 yards. It was the second-highest total ever for a schoolboy running back. He averaged nearly eight yards per carry, and scored an incredible 106 touchdowns. Rushing for 100 yards in a game is a mark of excellence that every running back strives for. Emmitt reached that lofty total in 45 of his 49 games at Escambia, including the last 28 in a row.

With a record such as that, it was no wonder that colleges across the country tried to recruit him. He finished in the top one hundred of his graduating class academically, so it was no surprise that he received so much attention. Ironically, one of the schools that was interested in him was the University of Miami. The school's head coach was

Emmitt Smith has always been at the center of media attention. Even in college, he was mobbed by reporters.

Jimmy Johnson, who would later be Emmitt's coach with the Cowboys.

Emmitt looked at offers from dozens of major schools. He eventually narrowed his choice to three—Auburn, Nebraska, and Florida. His mother had hoped he would choose Florida, since it was in the state. It also had a good academic reputation. In the end, Emmitt came to the same conclusion. The fall of 1987 saw him travel three hundred miles to Gainesville, where the school was located.

Florida held high hopes for its sensational young runner. At the college's annual Media Day, local writers referred to him as the school's "savior." Although he was flattered by such talk, Smith was mature enough not to let it go to his head. "I'm not anyone's savior," he politely informed the writers. "There's a lot of guys on this team who can play ball. I'm just here to play my hardest and help the Gators win."

Florida's head football coach, Galen Hall, tried to take some of the pressure off his freshman prospect. He did not start him in the team's first game of the year against Miami. Smith made a brief appearance in the last period. The Gators lost by a lopsided 31–4 score. The next week, against Tulsa, he rushed for 109 yards and scored two touchdowns. That was enough to convince Coach Hall that Smith could handle the pressure. He started the following week against Alabama, and sparked his team to a 23–14 upset victory. The 224 yards he gained on the ground that day broke the Gator's all-time record. It had been set more than half a century earlier.

Success followed upon success. By the seventh game of the year, Smith had surpassed the 1,000-yard mark in rushing. It was the fastest anyone had ever reached that level in the history of Division I-A college football. He finished the season with 1,341 yards, and eight 100-yard games. Florida ended the year with a 6–5 record. Smith was so impressive that he finished ninth in the voting for the Heisman Trophy. That prestigious award is given each year to the outstanding college football player in the country.

Smith's sophomore year at Florida was not as successful as his first. A new offensive coordinator joined the coaching staff. It took the players time to make adjustments. In addition, Smith suffered his first major injury. He stretched a ligament in his knee in the sixth game of the year against Memphis State. Although it hurt to miss time on the field, the injury helped bring across something his parents had always told him. "Football could end any moment," they said. "But your education will last your entire life." Taking these words to heart, Smith promised himself he would never take his schoolwork lightly.

Following four weeks of therapy, he returned to the field for the Gators' game against Georgia. His knee passed the test. Smith ran for 88 yards while wearing a knee brace. He finished out the rest of the year, but his statistics were down due to the time he missed. He finished with 988 yards rushing. Although this is a respectable total for most players, it was disappointing for him. He had never before failed to gain at least 1,000 yards in a season since he was a freshman in high school.

Even though the injury slowed Smith down, his reputation continued to grow. Louisiana State University coach Mike Archer said, "I knew he was something special when our players were still talking about him several days after we'd played him. They've played against a lot of great runners, and they haven't talked about them that way. Emmitt is something else."

Florida finished with a 6–5 record for the second consecutive season. The Gators then defeated Illinois, 14–10, in the All-American Bowl in Birmingham, Alabama. Smith

Busting through the line, Emmitt Smith breaks a tackle and heads upfield. From his high school days, through the 1996 season, Smith has never rushed for less than 900 yards in a season.

gained 159 yards in the game and scored two touchdowns. One was on a 55-yard run on the game's first play from scrimmage. Smith was named Florida's Most Valuable Player. Although it was gratifying to end the year with a victory, Smith had suffered through the most difficult football season of his young life. He did not know it at the time, but more hard times were yet to come.

Chapter 3

For a running back, the offensive coordinator on a football team can be just as important as the head coach. Whitey Jordan was hired for this position as Smith began his junior year at Florida. Right from the start, the two hit it off. Jordan placed more emphasis on the running game. The previous offensive coordinator had stressed passing.

Smith responded well to the new system. He continued to pile up 100-yard games. After a loss to Mississippi in the opener, Florida won its next four contests. A come-from-behind 16–13 win over Louisiana State at Louisiana's Tiger Stadium was the highlight of the streak.

Yet, just as the team seemed on its way to bigger and better things, a series of bombshells hit. Head coach Galen Hall announced his resignation on October 8. The players were stunned by the announcement. Defensive coordinator Gary Darnell was named interim coach. Rumors began to surface that the school was under investigation by the National Collegiate Athletic Association (NCAA) for rules violations.

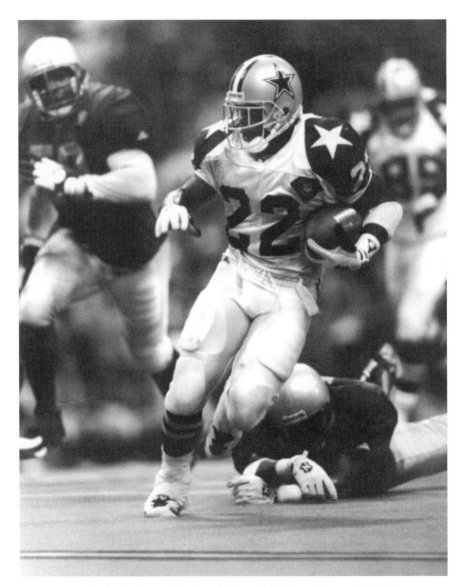

Emmitt Smith leaves this Detroit Lions defender with arms full of air as Smith looks to take on the next tackler. In Smith's junior year at the University of Florida, new offensive coordinator Whitey Jordan stressed the running game. With a running back like Smith, that's always a good idea.

In addition, the Gators' starting quarterback and backup quarterback were suspended for gambling.

Amazingly, the team continued to win. Despite nagging injuries, Smith ran for over 200 yards as Florida walloped Vanderbilt, 34–11. It was the team's fifth consecutive win. Even Whitey Jordan could not believe his star's performance. "He's leading us in rushing and receiving," he said, "and he's been hurt all year."

New Mexico came next. Smith came through with the most productive game of his college career. On October 21, he led Florida to a 27–21 victory by rushing for 316 yards and scoring three touchdowns. In the process, Smith broke fourteen school records. He now had 3,457 yards rushing for his career to go along with his 33 touchdowns.

The Gators won their seventh game in a row by defeating Kentucky, but then the magic ran out. Despite playing well, Florida lost its final three games of the year to Auburn, Georgia, and Florida State. A loss to Washington in the Freedom Bowl brought Florida's season to an end. Smith gained only 17 yards rushing to finish his year.

One final shock remained. Steve Spurrier had been hired as Florida's new head coach. Since the coach is allowed to choose his own assistants, this meant offensive coordinator Whitey Jordan would be leaving.

Under Jordan, Smith led the Southeastern Conference in rushing, and broke the school's all-time record. Smith began to wonder about his future at Florida. Did he want to play for a new head coach? Did he want to play for another offensive coordinator? Did he want to play for a school that might be given probation by the NCAA? Making his decision even harder was a new ruling made by the National Football League. Beginning with the 1990 draft, NFL teams would be allowed to draft college juniors, as well as seniors.

When Emmitt Smith left Florida after his junior year, he promised his mother that he would return to graduate. In 1996, Smith fulfilled that promise when he earned a degree in public recreation.

Smith's dream of playing professional football was beginning to win out. He did not make his final decision, however, until he discussed it with his mother. When she agreed with him, his mind was made up. He promised his mother he would come back to school to earn his degree, no matter how long it took. His mother knew he would keep his word. "He was always a determined child," she said. "All of my children have been determined. I like to think it's something that starts at home." Smith would fulfill his promise to his mother in 1996.

On January 31, 1990, Smith held a press conference. He announced that he was submitting his name for the draft. Although his family backed him, some people felt he was deserting the school. He even received hate mail from people who felt betrayed by his decision.

The National Football League draft was held in April. The Dallas Cowboys, Smith's favorite team as a youngster, had the twenty-first pick. Since Smith was one of the top players available, it seemed likely he would be taken before then. It was a shock, therefore, when he received a call from the Cowboys. They had traded to get the seventeenth pick in the draft. They were going to take him with it. Smith's dream was coming true. He was going to play professional football with the Dallas Cowboys of the NFL.

In 1990, the Cowboys were not the powerhouse team they are today. The year before, they won only one game against fifteen losses. Owner Jerry Jones and head coach Jimmy Johnson saw better days ahead. They wanted Smith to be an important part of the team's future. Smith was drafted even though some people questioned his size and speed. Johnson explained, "There were all these people saying, 'He's too slow,' or 'He's too small.' All I know is that every time I saw a film of him, he was running, 50, 60, 70, 80 yards for a touchdown. That looked pretty good to me." Things were starting to look up for the Cowboys.

Smith finished the semester at Florida, then went to Dallas. Training camp for the team began in mid-July. Smith's agent, Richard Howell, was still in the process of negotiating his contract. Following the draft, the Cowboys had announced that they had Smith rated as the fourth-best player in the draft. Therefore, his agent reasoned, he should get more money than a seventeenth pick. Talks dragged on. On September 4, just five days before the season was to begin, the two sides finally agreed to terms. Smith signed a contract that would pay him $3 million over three years.

Because of the contract problems, Cowboys' backfield coach Joe Brodsky did not think Smith was in shape for the season. In addition, offensive coordinator David Shula favored a passing game. Those two factors combined to limit Smith's playing time. Dallas won its opening game against the San Diego Chargers, but Smith contributed little. Coming off the bench, he carried the ball just two times and gained two yards. He started at tailback the next week against the New York Giants. The results were not much better. He carried only six times as the Cowboys were defeated.

Smith carried the ball a total of 28 times over the next two games. Two more losses convinced the Cowboys' coaching staff to change their game plan. As the team prepared for its game against the Tampa Bay Buccaneers, Smith was told, "Okay, Emmitt, you're getting the ball this Sunday."

The results were impressive. Smith carried the ball 23 times and gained a total of 121 yards. Dallas defeated the Bucs by a score of 14–10. The winning score came on a 14-yard touchdown run by Smith. He was pleasantly surprised at the turn of events. "I didn't expect them to hand me the ball as much as they did," he said.

Smith's playing time continued to increase throughout his rookie year.
By the end of the year, he was the Cowboys' leading rusher.

The following weeks, however, saw the team return to its passing game. The Cowboys won only one of their next five games. Smith got more and more frustrated. He finally went to the coaching staff and asked for more carries. With the team's record at 3–7, there was nothing to lose.

The Cowboys won their next four games as Smith played a bigger role in the offense. In a nationally televised contest against the Washington Redskins, he had his best game as a rookie. He gained 132 yards rushing and scored two touchdowns. In a 41–10 win over the Phoenix Cardinals, Smith scored four touchdowns, while carrying the ball 24 times. People began comparing him to former Cowboys running great Tony Dorsett.

With their record even at 7–7, the Cowboys still had a chance to make the playoffs. That opportunity quickly passed. Quarterback Troy Aikman was injured in the opening period of an important game against the Philadelphia Eagles. The Cowboys couldn't recover. They lost their final two games and finished the year at 7–9. This was a big improvement, however, over their 1–15 record of the previous season. They had narrowly missed becoming the first NFL team to go from a one-win season to the playoffs in the following year.

Smith finished the year with 937 yards rushing. That placed him tenth in the league, and first among all rookies. The Associated Press (AP) voted him the NFL Offensive Rookie of the Year. Many players would have been satisfied with such a season. Still, Smith knew he was capable of achieving even more.

Chapter 4

Emmitt Smith approached the 1991 season with a sense of optimism. David Shula had been demoted by Coach Jimmy Johnson. Norv Turner was hired as the new offensive coordinator. Turner had previously coached at the University of Southern California. The school had a reputation for developing great runners. Smith hoped that would be an advantage for him.

Cowboys' owner Jerry Jones also had high expectations for his club. "I don't believe in five-year, six-year, or seven-year plans," he said. "I feel like we are a couple of key players away from the Super Bowl, but we're trying to get those players now."

The first game of the year saw the Cowboys play the Cleveland Browns. It gave an indication of things to come. Smith carried the ball a career-high 32 times. He also caught six passes. No Dallas running back had ever touched the ball as many times in a game. The result was a 26–24 victory for the Cowboys.

The heavy workload took its toll on Smith's body. The

Emmitt Smith cheers on his teammates while the Cowboys' defense is on the field. Having good team spirit adds to the chemistry of the team.

next week, he drank a food supplement to give him extra energy. Unfortunately, it also made him sick to his stomach. He scored a touchdown on a 75-yard run early in the game. By halftime, he had rushed for 109 yards. In the second half, however, he only gained 3 more. The Washington Redskins defeated the Cowboys 33–31 to even Dallas's record.

The following week saw the Cowboys shut out by the Philadelphia Eagles. It was the ninth time in a row they had lost to their divisional rivals. The club bounced back to defeat the Phoenix Cardinals the next week by a 17–9 score. Early in the game, Smith scored on a 60-yard run. He finished the day with 182 yards gained on the ground. It was a new career high for him.

After four weeks of play, the Cowboys' record stood at 2–2. Smith's record was more impressive. He had already gained 450 yards rushing. For the first time in his brief career, he was the league leader in that category.

The Cowboys won their next three games, followed by a loss and another victory. At that point in the schedule, Dallas's record stood at 6–3. The next two weeks proved to be disastrous.

The Cowboys went to Houston to play the Oilers in the Astrodome. The teams played evenly for sixty minutes. Regulation time ended with the score tied, 23–23. With six minutes left in overtime, Smith committed a crucial mistake. A fumble gave the ball back to the Oilers. Quarterback Warren Moon drove his team down the field. A field goal gave Houston a 26–23 win.

Smith knew his fumble was costly. He had to try to put it behind him in order to prepare for the next week's game. The Cowboys' opponent was the Super Bowl champion New York Giants. The Giants players were looking to avenge their loss at Dallas earlier in the season. They played a tough game and defeated the Cowboys, 22–9. Smith fumbled two more times. Even though one of those came on a missed call by the referee, Smith still felt bad. Coach Johnson was not in a forgiving mood. "I don't know where your head is at today!" he hollered. "You better get it back here in this football game!"

With the team's record now at 6–5, the scolding was just what Smith needed. He couldn't afford to hang his head and feel sorry for himself.

The Cowboys flew to Washington for their next game. The Redskins, who would go on to win the Super Bowl, had not yet lost a game. Their 11–0 record was the best in the league. Dallas was unquestionably the underdog. Washington took an early 7–0 lead, but Smith's 32-yard run tied the score. A touchdown by rookie Alvin Harper gave Dallas a 14–7 lead at the half. With Smith running the ball time and again, the Cowboys held on to hand Washington its first defeat, 24–21. "A lot of people thought we were going to get crushed," said Smith. "It feels really good to know you proved all the experts wrong." Smith carried the ball 34 times for a total of 132 yards.

The only bad news for Dallas had to do with quarterback Troy Aikman. He injured his knee in the second half. It appeared he would miss the remainder of the regular season. Backup quarterback Steve Beuerlein performed well in his place, but the Cowboys knew they needed Smith even more than usual.

Four days later, on Thanksgiving, Smith ran 32 times in a victory over the Pittsburgh Steelers. He followed with big games against the New Orleans Saints, the Philadelphia Eagles, and the Atlanta Falcons. Dallas won each of those contests to end the season with a five-game winning streak. The team's 11–5 record was good enough to put it into the playoffs for the first time since 1985.

Emmitt Smith and Troy Aikman celebrate a Dallas touchdown. Aikman has been a major part of the Cowboys' success in the 1990s.

Emmitt Smith jokes with a teammate while taking a well-deserved rest.

Over the course of those last five games, Smith rushed an average of 30 times per game. Many wondered if his body would be able to take the punishment. Yet Smith seemed to thrive under the workload. By gaining 160 yards against Atlanta in the last game of the regular season, he reached 1,563 yards for the year. That was enough to give him the league rushing title for the first time. He was the leading ground gainer in the NFL at the young age of twenty-two.

The 11–5 record marked the Cowboys' first winning season in five years. The Washington Redskins finished first in their division. By finishing second, the Cowboys qualified for the playoffs as a wild card team. Their first opponent was the Chicago Bears.

The game was a defensive battle. The Cowboys came out on top, winning by a score of 17–13. Smith had a noteworthy performance. The Bears are one of the National Football League's oldest franchises. They had appeared in 27 postseason games dating back to 1932. In all that time, no back had ever rushed for 100 yards in a playoff game against them. Smith became the first to do so. He ran for 105 yards on 26 carries in the victory.

From Chicago, the Cowboys moved on to Detroit, where they played the Lions in the second round. It was there that their season came to a crashing halt. They were overmatched against the Lions and lost, 38–6. Smith was one of the few Dallas players to perform well in the losing effort. He gained 50 yards, and averaged more than five each time he carried the ball.

Following the end of the season, Smith made his second appearance in the Pro Bowl. This is the NFL's equivalent of baseball's All-Star Game. In his rookie year, he had been named to the game to replace an injured player. This time, he went because he was voted in. His sophomore season as a pro ended on this positive note.

Chapter 5

Optimism ran high in Dallas as the players prepared for the 1992 season. Norv Turner's system had done wonders. After having the worst offense in the NFL in 1990, the Cowboys finished ninth in the league in 1991. Smith had become the youngest player in league history to gain 1,500 yards rushing in a season. Wide receiver Michael Irvin led the NFL in receiving yardage. Quarterback Troy Aikman was completely recovered from the knee injury that caused him to miss several games in 1991. Everyone expected great things from the trio.

Prior to the start of the season, the Cowboys obtained defensive end Charles Haley in a trade with the San Francisco 49ers. Haley had been the National Football Conference's Defensive Player of the Year two years before. Safety Thomas Everett also joined the team in a trade with the Pittsburgh Steelers. All signs pointed to an improved defense to go along with the Cowboys' potent offense.

Dallas opened the regular season by playing host to the Washington Redskins. Offense and defense meshed perfectly. The Cowboys rolled over the defending Super Bowl

Michael Irvin picks up Emmitt Smith to congratulate him on another Cowboys' touchdown. Irvin blossomed into one of the league's premier receivers in 1991.

champions by a score of 23–10. Smith picked up where he left off the year before. He gained 140 yards rushing on 27 carries.

The second week almost proved to be disastrous. The Cowboys led the New York Giants, 34–0, in the third period. Perhaps the team got overconfident. The Giants mounted a furious comeback. They scared the Cowboys by pulling to within 34–28 when time ran out.

After that scare, Dallas defeated the Phoenix Cardinals for their third win in a row. All three wins were against Eastern Division foes. People began taking the Cowboys as serious contenders for the division title.

The Philadelphia Eagles were also undefeated. When Dallas came to Philadelphia for their next game, the Eagles were more than ready for them. Philadelphia led, 10–7, at halftime. After intermission, the Eagles put the game away. They scored 21 unanswered points for a 31–7 victory. The Cowboys knew they still had room for improvement.

They showed that improvement by winning their next five games. First they shut out the Seattle Seahawks, 27–0, followed by a 17–10 win over the Kansas City Chiefs. Although the team was 5–1 at this point, Smith had not been as productive as he had hoped to be. In those first six games, he had rushed for 100 yards only twice. All that changed in the Cowboys' 28–13 win over the Los Angeles Raiders. Smith carried time after time, piling up the yards. When the dust cleared, he had run for 152 yards and scored three touchdowns. "The way he cuts and slashes, he's awesome," said Raiders' defensive end Anthony Smith. The Cowboys now prepared for a rematch against the Eagles.

Dallas was too much for Philadelphia to handle. Smith rushed for 115 yards in the second half alone. He led the Cowboys to a 20–10 victory, gaining a total of 163 yards on

30 carries. Dallas reached the halfway point of the season with a record of 7–1. The team knew, however, that the second half of the season was most important. "You don't go to the Super Bowl winning the first half," said Smith. "You go by winning both halves."

The following week, the Cowboys were even more impressive. They pounded the Detroit Lions by a score of 37–3. By this point in the season, Smith had already scored 12 touchdowns for a total of 72 points. In comparison, the entire Seattle Seahawks team had scored only 56 points.

Dallas's five-game winning streak was ended by the Los Angeles Rams. The team got back on the right track by following with a win over the Cardinals. Although Dallas's record was now 9–2, the team knew it still faced a difficult part of its schedule. It could not assume the division race was over.

With Smith leading the way, the Cowboys proceeded to soundly defeat the New York Giants on Thanksgiving Day, 30–3. Dallas led 9–3 at halftime. In the third period, Smith scored on touchdowns of 26 and 68 yards to end the suspense.

The Cowboys defeated the Broncos in Denver, then lost to the Washington Redskins the following week. The game was decided on a controversial call by the referees. What should have been an incomplete pass was ruled a fumble. Smith recovered the ball in the end zone. He tried to hand off to tight end Alfredo Roberts, but the ball came loose once again. This time, the Redskins recovered for the winning touchdown.

The next week, the Cowboys and Smith got back on track. Dallas defeated the Atlanta Falcons, 41–17. Smith gained 174 yards rushing, and scored two touchdowns. More importantly for Dallas, the victory allowed the Cowboys to clinch the NFC Eastern Division title.

Emmitt Smith slashes to his right to avoid a would-be tackler. Smith ran for over 1,700 yards in 1992, to lead the NFL in rushing for the second straight season.

The regular season ended with a win over the Chicago Bears. Smith once again gained over 100 yards. In the process, he won his second consecutive rushing title, gaining a total of 1,713 yards. He edged out running back Barry Foster of the Pittsburgh Steelers. Smith's efforts were rewarded when he was again named as a starter in the NFL Pro Bowl.

By finishing with a mark of 13–3, Dallas set a team record for wins in the regular season. Coach Jimmy Johnson, however, was not satisfied. "It's been a good year for us," he said, "but we have a lot of football left to be played." The Cowboys began to prepare for the playoffs.

Dallas's first opponent was the Philadelphia Eagles. It was the first playoff game played in Dallas in ten years. Before the game, Philadelphia safety Andre Waters issued a threat to Smith. "Two of us are going to walk on the field," he said, "but only one of us is going to walk off. They're going to have to carry him off." The Cowboys proceeded to trounce their archrivals, 34–10. Smith gained 114 yards rushing, and scored one touchdown. After the game, Waters was asked about Smith. "What can I say?" he replied. "Today he showed he's a great running back."

The win put the Cowboys in the conference championship game. Their opponent, the San Francisco 49ers, was considered by many to be the best team in the league. They were no match for Dallas that day, however. The score was tied, 10–10, at halftime. In the second half, the youthful Cowboys did everything right. Dallas won by a final score of 30–20. Smith rushed for 114 yards, caught seven passes, and scored two more touchdowns. The 49ers were impressed by his play. "You go to a big-time player in a big game like this," said linebacker Keith DeLong. "He was big time. We couldn't

Emmitt Smith celebrates a touchdown during Super Bowl XXVII. Smith ran for 108 yards in the game, as the Cowboys won their first Super Bowl in fifteen years.

stop him, especially in the second half." Dallas was on its way to Super Bowl XXVII.

More than 98,000 fans were in the stands at the Rose Bowl in Pasadena, California, on January 31, 1993. The Cowboys were meeting the Buffalo Bills for the championship of the National Football League. Dallas was playing in its sixth Super Bowl, and its first in fourteen years. Buffalo was playing in its third consecutive title game. The Bills had lost to the Washington Redskins and New York Giants the previous two seasons. They entered the game with victory on their minds, even though Dallas was favored to win.

With his appearance, Smith became the first rushing leader ever to play in a Super Bowl. The Cowboys knew that a good game from him would increase their chances for victory. Since joining Dallas, Smith had run for 100 or more yards in a game 20 times. The Cowboys had won 19 of those games. "He's the final piece in our puzzle," said Dallas guard Nate Newton. "As long as he runs well, Troy [Aikman] stays poised. And then nobody can stop us."

The Bills scored first to take an early 7–0 lead. Still the Cowboys were not to be denied. Dallas's defense caused the Bills to make nine turnovers, a Super Bowl record. The Cowboys scored time after time. Smith rushed for 108 yards and caught six passes. He scored a touchdown on a 10-yard run in the fourth period. Quarterback Troy Aikman also played a magnificent game. He completed 22 of 30 passes, and threw for four touchdowns. When the dust finally cleared, Dallas was victorious by a score of 52–17. Aikman was voted the game's Most Valuable Player, and the Cowboys were champions of the football world.

Chapter 6

When Smith was drafted out of college, he signed a three-year contract with the Cowboys. In those first three seasons, he led the league in rushing two times. He appeared in the Pro Bowl three times. His play helped Dallas win the Super Bowl. Like anyone else, he wanted to be paid what he felt he was worth.

During the 1992 season, team owner Jerry Jones told Smith he felt he was a better player than Barry Sanders of the Detroit Lions. He then offered him the same amount of money as Sanders. Smith turned down the offer. He wanted to be paid for his accomplishments. His goal was to be the highest-paid non-quarterback in the league.

Because of his years in the league, Smith was eligible for restricted free agency. This meant that any team in the league could offer him a contract. The Cowboys, however, had the right to sign him by matching that offer.

In July, Jones made another offer. Smith again turned it down. Training camp was just around the corner. The two sides were far apart in the negotiations. Jones began saying negative things about Smith in the papers. "Emmitt Smith is a

Smith missed the start of the 1993 season because of a contract dispute. Is it possible that Smith could have become a violinist if things didn't work out?

luxury, not a necessity, for the Cowboys." "The Cowboys can win a Super Bowl without Emmitt Smith." Smith felt Jones was underestimating his value to the team.

Strangely enough, no other team even made an offer for the star running back. "We've talked about him," said Denver Broncos coach Wade Phillips, "but we feel like they're going to match whatever we offer. . . . We're just not going to fall for it."

The beginning of the season got closer, but little changed. Tensions built up during training camp. The players sided with Smith in his dispute with management. Jones increased his offer, but not enough to get Smith to sign. Coach Jimmy Johnson seemed resigned to the fact that Smith would not be with the club. Said Johnson, "I can't think of what would happen to our offense without Emmitt." He would soon find out.

The Cowboys opened the year against the Redskins. Without Smith, Dallas lost to Washington, 35–16. A week later, a 13–10 defeat by the Buffalo Bills in a rematch of the Super Bowl dropped the Cowboys' record to 0–2. Morale on the team was at a low point. Michael Irvin said, "If we want to beat the Goliaths, we've got to have a great slingshot. Emmitt's the rock in our slingshot." Irvin even wore Smith's uniform number twenty-two on his helmet in support of his teammate. Owner Jones finally seemed to realize how much the Cowboys needed Smith. The following Thursday, Smith agreed to a four-year contract for $13.6 million. It was the contract Smith had been looking for two months earlier. The holdout was over. It was time to get back to work.

Dallas defeated Phoenix that Sunday for its first win of the year. In one half of play, Smith rushed for 45 yards in the 17–10 victory. "Just like the old days," said teammate Nate Newton. The Cowboys were back.

Emmitt Smith and Michael Irvin emerge from the end zone after a
Cowboys' touchdown. During Smith's contract dispute, Irvin wore
Smith's number on his helmet to show Smith's importance to the team.

Smith started against Green Bay in Dallas the following week. The hometown fans went crazy as the Cowboys won again, 36–14. Smith scored his first touchdown of the season on a 22-yard run. Dallas's record now stood at 2–2. The Cowboys were back on the right track. Smith's chances for a third consecutive rushing title did not appear good, however. No one had ever led the league in rushing while missing two games of the season. Still, Smith did not give up hope. "To get a title after all this would really be something special," he said. "I'm sure the odds are way, way up there. But I wouldn't bet against me."

The next month-and-a-half saw the Cowboys win all five of their games. The seven-game winning streak put Dallas back on top in the NFC East.

The game against Philadelphia was a noteworthy one for Smith. In a heavy rainstorm, he carried the ball 30 times. He gained 237 yards rushing to set a new Cowboys' record. It was also the sixth-best mark in National Football League history.

The next week proved to be a bad one for Dallas. The lowly Atlanta Falcons surprised them with a 27–14 victory. Just before halftime, Smith was struck on the right thigh by a Cowboys' lineman. Although no bones were broken, he sustained a deep bruise. Playing a Thanksgiving Day game against Miami that Thursday, Smith ran for only 51 yards. The Dolphins won, 16–14, on a field goal with less than 15 seconds left to play. The loss dropped Dallas's record to 7–4.

As is often the case, adversity brought out the best in Smith and the Cowboys. Dallas bounced back to defeat the Eagles, with Smith gaining 172 yards. They then rolled over the Minnesota Vikings, 37–20, New York Jets, 28–7, and Washington Redskins, 38–3. In the Washington game, Smith gained 153 yards. It put him at the top of the NFL rushing category for the first time all season.

The final game of the regular season pitted the Cowboys against the New York Giants. Whoever won would have a week off in the first round of the playoffs. They would also have the home-field advantage when they did play.

In a thrilling contest, Dallas defeated New York in overtime by a score of 16–13. Smith gave one of the most outstanding individual performances in the history of the league. He carried the ball 32 times and gained 168 yards rushing. In addition, he caught ten passes for 61 yards and one touchdown. In the drive for the winning score, Smith got the ball nine times in 11 plays. He gained 41 of the team's 52 yards on the drive.

The most amazing thing of all was that most of this was achieved after Smith suffered a severe shoulder separation in the second quarter. He had been slammed to the turf by Giants safety Greg Jackson after making a 46-yard run. Somehow he continued to play. Even his teammates were astounded. "Emmitt was hurting, he was done," said guard Kevin Grogan. "He sucked it up for his boys. I don't know how he did it."

His 168 yards rushing gave Smith 1,486 for the year. It was enough to earn him a third consecutive rushing title. Only three other players had accomplished that feat in the history of the NFL. Shortly after, he was named the league's Most Valuable Player. He became the first Dallas player ever to win the award.

The Cowboys moved into the postseason with their star running back injured. The injury, however, would not keep Smith on the sidelines. "There's no way they'll keep me out of it," he said.

The Cowboys won their first-round game against the Green Bay Packers, 27–17. Smith gained only 60 yards

Emmitt Smith shows his emotions after a Cowboys' victory.

rushing. It was obvious he was in pain. However, no further damage was done to his shoulder.

The next week saw the Cowboys play perhaps their toughest opponent—the San Francisco 49ers. Dallas coach Jimmy Johnson surprised everyone. On the Thursday before the game, he went on radio and guaranteed that the Cowboys would defeat the 49ers. Perhaps his outrageous statement inspired his players. Dallas scored first on Smith's 5-yard run. San Francisco tied the score at 7–7. The Cowboys scored the next three touchdowns, giving them a 28–7 lead at the half. Quarterback Troy Aikman suffered a concussion in the second half, but Dallas held on for a 38–21 victory.

The Cowboys were going to the Super Bowl for the second year in a row. Smith had established his reputation in no uncertain terms. Chris Mortensen, columnist for *The Sporting News*, wrote, "It is time to give Smith his due. He is the NFL's best back. Sanders and Buffalo's Thurman Thomas fall in line after Smith. No disgrace there. But Smith is the best."

Emmitt Smith added to his reputation by putting on an amazing performance in Super Bowl XXVIII. His 132 yards rushing and two touchdowns helped lead the Cowboys to a 30–13 victory over the Buffalo Bills. It was the Cowboys' second consecutive championship. For his contribution, Smith was named the game's Most Valuable Player.

Chapter 7

Some players might suffer a letdown after having a year like Smith did in 1993. How could you improve upon being named Most Valuable Player in both the regular season and the Super Bowl? Smith's desire to be the best was all the incentive he needed. "There's so much more I need to accomplish," he said. "I have so much room to grow, both as a player and as a person. If you're satisfied, you're finished. You can never be satisfied."

Shortly after the Super Bowl victory, Norv Turner left the Cowboys to take the head coaching job with Washington. The next month, Smith underwent successful surgery to repair his injured shoulder. The biggest bombshell of all, however, was the resignation of head coach Jimmy Johnson in late March. Owner Jerry Jones had had several highly publicized disagreements with his coach. He now brought in former Oklahoma coach Barry Switzer to replace him.

Switzer guided Dallas to a 12–4 record during the 1994 regular season. Smith got off to the fastest start of his career.

After three games, he had accounted for 404 yards rushing. Injuries, however, proved to be his undoing.

Smith led the league with 22 touchdowns scored. He lost the rushing title, however. Barry Sanders of Detroit and Chris Warren of Seattle both surpassed his total of 1,484 yards gained on the ground. Smith was hampered by a hamstring muscle he pulled in a December game against the New Orleans Saints. "It's been a tough, physical year," he said. "It seems as if something is always hurting."

After receiving a first-round bye in the playoffs, the Cowboys beat the Green Bay Packers, 35–9, to advance to the NFC title game. There, they were defeated by the San Francisco 49ers by a score of 38–28. Smith was held to 74 yards rushing by the 49ers' defense. The Cowboys' dream of a third straight Super Bowl victory came crashing down. San Francisco went on to defeat the San Diego Chargers in Super Bowl XXIX.

The following year saw Smith and the Cowboys bounce back in a big fashion. Smith was determined to prove he had shaken the effects of his injuries of the previous year. "You haven't seen me run yet," he said. "This season I'll run like I need to run."

To bolster its defense, Dallas signed premier defensive back Deion Sanders. Although this was a significant move, opposing players knew that Smith was still the key to the Cowboys' season. "I think they can win the Super Bowl without Deion," said tight end Shannon Sharpe of the Denver Broncos. "What sets them apart is Emmitt Smith."

In the opening game of the 1995 season, the Cowboys played the New York Giants. On the first offensive play from scrimmage, quarterback Troy Aikman handed the ball to Smith. Smith took off and did not stop running until he reached the end zone. His first carry of the season resulted in a 60-yard touchdown run.

He proceeded to pile up yards at a phenomenal rate. Smith gained more than 100 yards in a game eleven times. Before spraining his knee in a Thanksgiving Day game against the Kansas City Chiefs, Smith was on pace for a 2,000-yard season. He finished the year with 1,773 yards gained to lead the league for the fourth time in his career. He also set a National Football League record by scoring 25 touchdowns. His 150 points led the league, as did his 2,148 total yards. During the regular season, his running and pass-catching accounted for an incredible 40 percent of the Cowboys' total yards from scrimmage. His feats on the field continued to amaze his teammates. "When you think Emmitt has reached his peak," said guard Nate Newton, "all of a sudden he goes off and does something just a little better."

In the NFC title game against Green Bay, Smith rushed 35 times for 150 yards. He also scored three touchdowns. Dallas won by a score of 38–27 to advance to the Super Bowl for the third time in four years.

The powerful Pittsburgh Steelers were the Cowboys' opponents in the Super Bowl. The Cowboys gave Switzer his first title with a 27–17 win over the AFC champions. Smith ran for 49 yards against the Steelers. He raced for two touchdowns, including one with less than four minutes left in the game. The score clinched the victory for the Cowboys. Smith had his third championship ring in five years.

During the offseason, Smith's contract was on his mind. With one year left to go on it, Smith was scheduled to become a free agent after the 1996 season. He wanted to remain with the Cowboys, but wasn't sure what owner Jerry Jones had in mind. Talks progressed through the summer. Jones spoke optimistically. "[Smith] is going to spend the major part or

Emmitt Smith sweeps to the outside during Super Bowl XXX. The Cowboys defeated the Steelers, 27–17, to win their third Super Bowl in four years.

all of his career here," he said. "We have planned too long with our other contracts not to sign him and allow him to be a free agent."

Jones proved true to his word. In August, a new deal was announced. Smith would receive an incredible $42.5 million over eight years. Included in that amount was a signing bonus of $10.5 million. The money reflected his status as the premier running back in the league.

The new contract did not affect Smith's attitude toward the game. "To me," he said, "football is a means to another end. It's an opportunity to play the game you loved as a kid, but it's also an opportunity to open doors to other opportunities." The money helped him plan for his life after football. Among the businesses he was developing were a sports collectibles store and a communications corporation.

A good bit of his money went toward his charitable enterprises. The Sickle Cell Anemia Foundation, the Salvation Army, the Battered and Abused Children's Foundation, and the I Have a Dream Foundation have all benefited from Smith's time and funds. It's one of the ways he has been able to give something back to the community. "I'm more proud of that than anything else he's done," said Smith's dad.

On the football field, the 1996 season was a trying one for Smith. An ankle injury hampered him through most of the year. His rushing totals dropped significantly. Sportswriters hinted that hundreds of carries over the years had finally taken their toll. The Cowboys floundered early, and the Washington Redskins jumped into first place in the division.

Dallas battled back, however, and so did Smith. On Thanksgiving Day, he ran for 155 yards and scored three touchdowns in a victory over the first-place Redskins. This gave him more than 10,000 yards rushing for his career. Only eleven other running backs had reached that mark before him.

The performance was Smith's way of answering his critics. "To hear all that negative stuff," he said, "that people were saying I was on the back of my career, it really cut me deep."

The Cowboys moved into a tie for first place in the NFC East. They later clinched their fifth straight NFC East title with a 12–6 win over the New England Patriots. The injuries were taking their toll, however. Smith sat out the team's final game of the regular season. He finished the year with 1,204 yards rushing, the eighth-highest total in the league.

Coach Barry Switzer knew his star was suffering. "He doesn't have the quickness he has had in the past," he said. "He's obviously bothered by something. His ankle has been hurting."

With Smith at less than 100 percent, the Cowboys were in trouble. Still, they managed one final flash of greatness. The Cowboys defeated the Minnesota Vikings in the opening round of the playoffs by a 40–15 score. Smith ran for 116 yards and scored two touchdowns.

The team's offense had fallen off considerably. In 1995, the team ranked fifth in total offense in the league; in 1996, they were 24th. Injuries and suspensions to key players hurt the team's morale. The Cowboys lost their next game to the Carolina Panthers by a score of 26–17. The disappointing season came to an end.

Despite all the negatives, 1996 was a year Smith will never forget. The most memorable moment of all occurred before the season even started.

When he had left college after his junior year, Smith had promised his mother that he would continue to work to get his degree. Now, six years later, he reached that goal. In early May, he graduated from the University of Florida with a bachelor of science degree in public recreation. Earning a degree had been an important goal of Smith's for some time.

From left to right are legendary running backs Earl Campbell, Tony Dorsett, Walter Payton, and Emmitt Smith. One day, Smith hopes to break Payton's record for the most rushing yards in a career.

The achievement had nothing to do with money or contracts. "I always felt a little hypocritical talking to kids," he said, "when I hadn't accomplished my academic goals myself. Now I won't be lying."

Hard work has brought Smith fame and money. His deeds on and off the field have reflected the lessons taught to him by his parents. They are lessons he has tried to pass on to others. As he once said, "If you have a good, clean image and are performing on the field and are able to get your point across, you'll do fine."

Career Statistics

YEAR	TEAM	RUSHING				PASS RECEIVING			
		Carries	Yards	Avg.	TDs	Rec.	Yards	Avg.	TDs
1990	Dallas	241	937	3.9	11	24	228	9.5	0
1991	Dallas	365	1,563	4.3	12	49	258	5.3	1
1992	Dallas	373	1,713	4.6	18	59	335	5.7	1
1993	Dallas	283	1,486	5.3	9	57	414	7.3	1
1994	Dallas	368	1,484	4.0	21	50	341	6.8	1
1995	Dallas	377	1,773	4.7	25	62	375	6.0	0
1996	Dallas	327	1,204	3.7	12	47	249	5.3	3
Totals		2,334	10,160	4.4	108	348	2,200	6.3	7

Avg.=Average   **Rec.**=Receptions
TDs=Touchdowns

61

Where to Write Emmitt Smith:

Mr. Emmitt Smith
c/o Dallas Cowboys
Cowboys Center
One Cowboys Parkway
Irving, TX 75063

On the Internet at: http://www.nfl.com/players/

Index